C000174862

SWANSEA
Turns Back Time

SWANSEA
Turns Back Time

by David Roberts

South Wales
Evening Post

BRYNGOLD
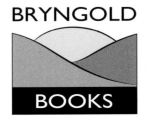
BOOKS

First published in Great Britain in 2004 by
Bryngold Books Ltd.,
Golden Oaks, 98 Brynau Wood, Cimla,
Neath, South Wales, SA11 3YQ.

© **David Roberts 2004**

All rights reserved. No part of this publication may be reproduced, stored in a retrieval system, or transmitted in any for, or by any means, electronic, mechanical, photocopying, recording, or otherwise without the prior permission, in writing, of the copyright holder, nor be otherwise circulated in any form or binding or cover other than that in which it is published and without a similar condition being imposed on the subsequent publisher.

ISBN 0 9547859 0 8

Printed in Wales by
Dinefwr Press, Rawlings Road,
Llandybie, Carmarthenshire, SA18 3YD.

Contents

An appreciation

Swansea Turns Back Time would not have been made possible without the valued assistance of readers of the South Wales Evening Post and the many residents of Swansea, past and present, who so willingly submitted their own cherished personal images of days gone by. However small their contribution it is just as valuable in making this a book that is for the people and by the people.
Particular thanks for their assistance are due to:
Cheryl Roberts
David Beynon, Gerald Gabb
David and Gay Mitchell
Michael and Diane Trow
Mayville Blay, Carol Darracott
Clive Cockings, Gay Davies
Marilyn Evans, Sylvia Floyd
Steve Phillips, Les Saunders
Robin Wayne, John Hutchins
Terry and Jill Quick, Roy Kneath
Huw Evans and Simmons Aerofilms.
Thanks also to Emyr Nicholas and staff at Dinefwr Press

For details of how you can play a part in this valuable ongoing pictorial archive telephone 01639 643961. All contributions for the next publication will be welcomed and returned after use.

Foreword

SWANSEA stands poised on the brink of a new era in its long history. Ambitious development plans will in time see a dramatic transformation with the creation of new waterfront communities and business districts.

What better time, then, to enjoy the latest book of nostalgic photographs produced by Evening Post journalist David Roberts.

Through its pages we can capture moments from the ever-changing face of a busy and thriving city. Half-forgotten landmarks are remembered, and lost views recaptured through this unique collection of photographs.

They carry us from the era of horse-drawn transport in quiet streets to the bustling city of today. How many of us, who have to put up with the frustrations of daily rush hour traffic, will cast an envious eye over the pages that are dedicated to the network of suburban railway lines that once ran throughout the area. What would today's planners give to have them back!

The business and social life of Swansea from the start of the previous century is represented inside this book. Once more, David Roberts deserves our thanks for compiling this record, so that all of us who have enjoyed his previous volumes can again explore the highways and byways of our yesterdays.

Spencer Feeney
Editor
South Wales Evening Post

Fast forward to a new identity

INTENT on adopting the mantle of a truly cosmopolitan European city, fast-paced twenty first Century Swansea has its eyes focused more clearly than ever on change and it is difficult to glance in a direction where this is not easy to witness.

Exciting new developments spell hope and fresh prosperity for the future but also mean that Dylan Thomas's ugly, lovely town is these days as much a candidate for the pages of books as his imagery-packed poetry.

Parts of the fabric of the community he held so dear still survive and will always fascinate those who take the time and trouble to seek them out, but the role they played in creating its true character fades unavoidably with the passing of each year.

Almost every aspect of city life is being bombarded with significant new projects of landmark proportions – sport, shopping, transport, education, housing, entertainment and work. These include the new stadium at White Rock, Castle Quays retail scheme, High Street station facelift, dockland regeneration, the Salubrious Place complex and the new national waterfront museum.

This rapid change of character, with bigger and more impressive projects following one after another often sweeps away that with which we were comfortable and familiar.

It is therefore important to the memory of the way we were to capture images of the old – the people, the places the streets and the scenery – before they make way for the new. Swansea Turns Back Time reflects them all. It looks at almost every aspect of the lives of those who have lived in the city, their priorities, their labours and their cultural and leisure interests. Its images, drawn from the people themselves, sum up much of what has gone before, reflect on its importance and mean that we will not forget.

Those who know and love Swansea will harbour their own reasons for believing that the city is unique, but even though change is both inescapable and inevitable they will surely be united in the view of Dylan Thomas when he described it as 'still the best place.' They will agree that is something that holds true to this day.

David Roberts, 2004.

CITY OF CHANGE

Crowds gather to watch a ceremony marking the laying of the foundation stone of St Mary's Church, May 19, 1896. The top of the Ben Evans department store is visible in the distance.

Oxford Street, looking away from the city centre shortly after the opening of the new market with its impressive, domed entrance, 1897. The picture was taken at the junction with Waterloo Street.

High Street at its junction with Prince of Wales Road, 1904. The Palace Theatre, built in 1888 as a traditional music hall is clearly visible on the right hand side. Now a Grade II listed building it is one of just two purpose built music halls left standing in the whole of the United Kingdom.

The view down High Street towards the railway station with the Palace Theatre dominating the left of the scene, 1904.

The inside of St Mary's Church with its stained glass windows in the early 1900s. The church was destroyed by wartime aerial bombardment in the Three Nights Blitz of February 1941, but was rebuilt and re-opened in 1959.

Castle Square, surveyed by the statue of industrialist Sir Henry Hussey Vivian, 1904. The Castle Hotel with its impressive pavement portico is on the left and further along the Ben Evans department store towers over the scene. The statue now stands in St David's Square, near St Mary's Church.

Oxford Street, 1904, with the impressive market entrance towering above. The original David Evans department store – opened in 1899 is in the centre distance.

The Ben Evans department
store, with its interesting
architectural styling,
dominates this 1904 view of
Castle Square at the top of
Wind Street.

Walter Road from its
junction with St James
Crescent, looking towards
the city centre, 1904.

An intriguing panorama of High Street, looking towards its railway station, 1906.

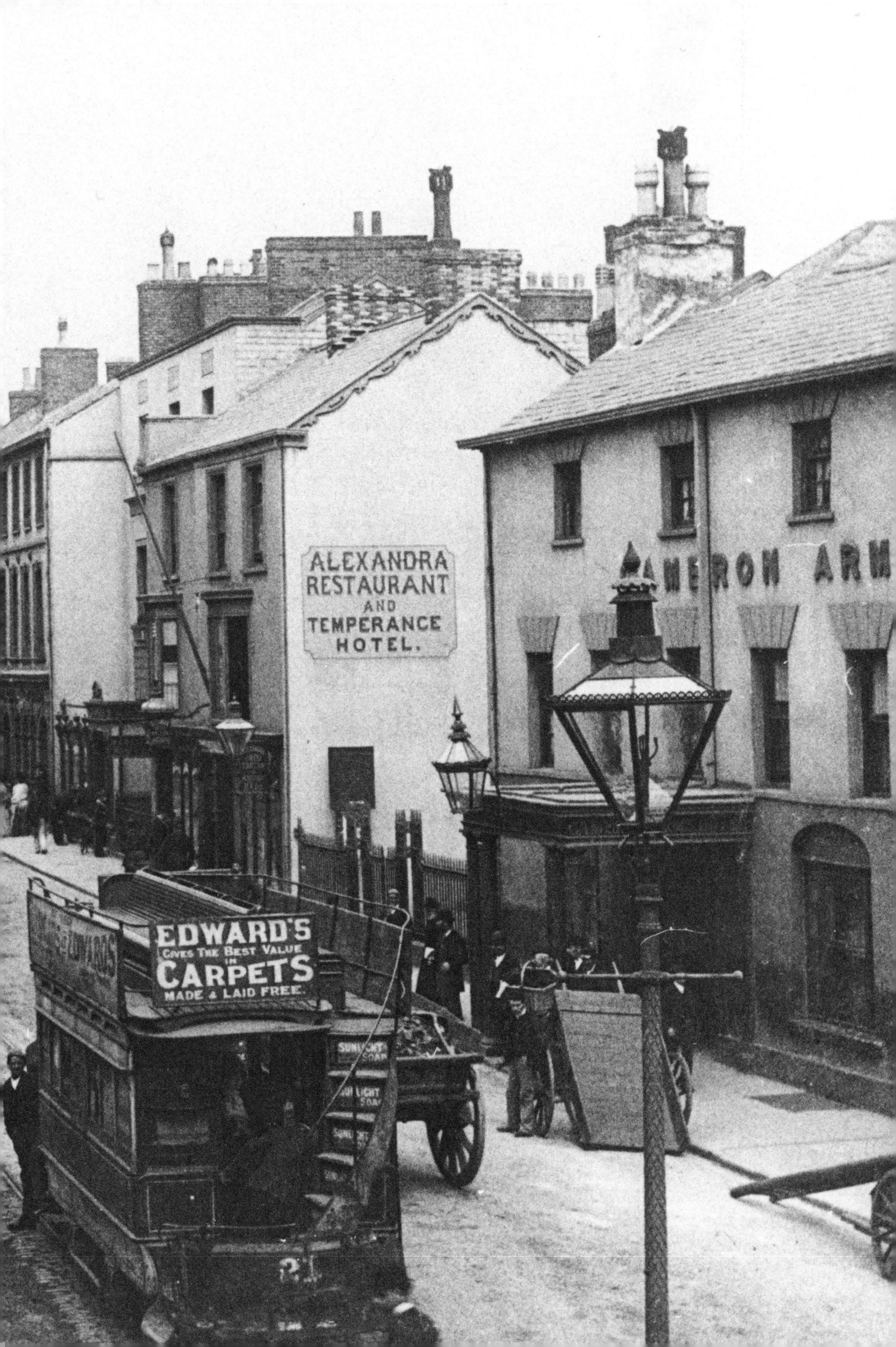
ALEXANDRA RESTAURANT AND TEMPERANCE HOTEL.
AMERON ARM
EDWARD'S GIVES THE BEST VALUE IN CARPETS MADE & LAID FREE.
SUNLIGHT SOAP

High Street, 1905. This point formed the terminus for the trams that shuttled to and from Cwmbwrla.

Mature trees and tramlines fill this Walter Road scene in 1905.

Oxford Street, looking eastwards with the tower of the imposing main market entrance in the background, 1905. The Empire Theatre – opened in 1900 – is on the right. John S. Brown, on both sides, sold bikes, hardware and installed electricity.

Looking eastwards along Oxford Street towards Temple Street, and beyond, the offices of the Cambria Daily Leader Newspaper, later the South Wales Evening Post, 1907.

A summer's day in 1910 on Mumbles Road, near The Slip where Swansea's trams linked with the Mumbles Railway. The Bay View Hotel stands right on the junction with St Helen's Road.

The Theophilus store was one of the main retail attractions of Oxford Street. It stood on its corner with Goat Street. 1907.

The Castle restaurant run by R E Jones in Castle Street was a popular rendezvous for diners. It is pictured here in the 1920s.

There was an interesting mix of architectural styles in the old town as this 1920s picture taken where Wind Street met Castle Bailey shows.

The imposing main façade of Swansea market makes its presence felt in this 1920s Oxford Street scene.

Looking up High Street from its junction with College Street, towards the Lewis Lewis department store, 1920s.

Wind Street in the mid-1920s.

With the tramlines gone and High Street yet to suffer from the aerial bombardment of the Second World War, this was how it looked in early 1939.

The Brunswick Arms on the corner of Caswell Street and Duke Street, 1930.

The forecourt of High Street station in the mid-1920s. The Grand Hotel was built on the site of the buildings on the right.

Heathfield Street, much of which was destroyed by the Three Night's Blitz of wartime, February 1941, presents a more peaceful scene in the mid-1930s when this view was captured. Today it forms part of the Kingsway.

The main entrance of the South Wales Evening Post office, Castle Bailey, in June 1941. As the arrowed sign suggests, the Castle cinema, a popular venue for film-goers, was alongside.

The ruins and the rubble that was Oxford Street as it appeared in the mid-1940s — the ravages of wartime bombing still much in evidence.

Looking across the city centre towards the castle and Wind Street, after the clearance of wartime bombing rubble, 1947. These large open areas or bomb sites as they were referred to were eventually redeveloped, but in post-war Swansea many of them served as convenient car parks.

New roads were the fist visible sign that Swansea was beginning to emege from the desolation of the Second World War. This was the Kingsway roundabout in 1950. Mount Pleasant chapel can be seen on the left and the Dragon Hotel, now the Holiday Inn, rose up on the site behind the double decker bus.

This view would be impossible today. Taken in the late 1940s it reveals the full sweep of Castle Buildings, Castle Street, albeit badly damaged by wartime bombing.

The majestic sweep of Victoria Park leads up to Swansea Guildhall, 1950.

A United Welsh bus company single deck Albion service vehicle heads along Oystermouth Road, passing the carriage sidings of the Swansea Victoria railway station, mid-1950s. The track of the Mumbles Railway can be seen alongside.

Three South Wales Transport double decker buses head down an unusually quiet High Street during July 1955.

Construction work on the Littlewoods department store in High Street, nears completion July 1955. The company later relocated to St Mary's Square.

Shoppers wait to catch their buses home at temporary stopping places created near the Kingsway roundabout during post-war redevelopment. The Kingsway can be seen in the background, 1955.

Rising from the ashes . . . rebuilding work underway on the roof of St Mary's Church. 1956.

The old and the new in Oxford Street, mid-1950s. The buildings behind this United Welsh double decker bus represent post-war Swansea rising from the ashes of wartime bombardment, while to the front of the vehicle can be seen the walls of the old market hall. Everything within them was destroyed in the blitz.

Construction work underway on Beau Nash House, Caer Street, 1957.

Looking Westwards along The Kingsway, 1962.

Castle Bailey, showing the offices of the South Wales Evening Post and Herald of Wales, looking towards Castle Street and Castle Buildings, 1962.

A South Wales transport AEC Regal III double decker bus pulls out of Caer Street into Princess Way, with Castle Gardens in the background, late 1950s.

The site in Adelaide Street, now occupied by the South Wales Evening Post building, as it was in the early 1960s.

The uppermost part of High Street, below today's busy Dyfatty traffic light junction looking down towards High Street railway station in the mid-1960s.

Oystermouth Road, between the Bay View Hotel and the Slip bridge, mid-1960s.

The caravans of travellers who converged on the empty land alongside the former Weaver's flour mill, in 1972. Sainsbury's supermarket and its car park was later built on the site.

Looking down from the corner of Castle Gardens into Wind Street, mid-1960s.

Excavation work on the site of the former Mackworth Hotel, High Street looking towards Orchard Street and the former Central Police Station, mid-1970s.

St Helen's Road, looking towards The Kingsway, early October, 1972. The YMCA building is on the left.

Castle Gardens with Caer Street's Beau Nash
House and Wind Street behind, mid 1970s.

Mount Pleasant maternity and geriatric hospital,
December 1974.

James Street, Swansea, now vanished under
redevelopment, September 1976.

An interesting early 1980s panorama of Swansea streets and terraces from the top of the city's Guildhall.

Oxford Street School, 1978. It was opened on August 26, 1848 and closed in 1969.

Castle Street viewed from High Street, with the Princess House office block in the background, 1982.

The old and new buildings of Swansea Institute blend effortlessly in this view up Mount Pleasant, early 1980s.

The former British Transport Docks Board offices, Adelaide Street, early 1980s, now the city's luxury, five-star Morgan's Hotel.

Looking across Orchard Street dual carriageway towards the Oldway House office development, early 1980s.

High Street's Oldway House office complex towers over the background
of this fascinating view from west to east across Swansea city centre.
The mid-1980s picture was taken from the Guildhall Clock Tower.

A July 1983 aerial view showing Swansea Leisure Centre, the South Dock marina and beyond it land that became the site for a whole string of maritime quarter apartment blocks. Much development has taken place since.

The canopy of David Evans department store, Princess Way, provides welcome shade on a warm summer afternoon, early 1980s.

The impressive central reading area of Swansea Reference Library, Alexandra Road, 1985.

The steel skeleton of Plantasia rises up at its North Dock site amid development of the Parc Tawe shopping complex, 1988.

Victoria Road, with Swansea Leisure Centre in the background and York Chambers, seemingly surrounded by parked cars in the centre, 1989. It is now the site of a hotel and cinema development with multi-storey car park behind.

Construction work on the River Tawe barrage, 1989, near the entrance to the marina lock gates.

MEET THE PEOPLE

Most of the members of the extended Morris family gather outside Morris Farm on Kilvey Hill, the home of grandparents Sarah and William Morris, centre, 1920.

The annual dinner of the Swansea and District Motorist's Fellowship League was held at the Hotel Metropole, 1937. Among guests was Mayor of Swansea, Councillor Richard Henry.

Princess Mary, the Princess Royal attends a rally of Glamorgan Girl Guides at Singleton Park, 1932.

The carnival queens and their attendants at Mumbles, in the summer of 1931.

Members of the Swansea Federation of Boys Clubs with their organisers and civic dignitaries at a summer camp, 1936.

Participants in the Band of Hope concert staged at Ebenezer Presbyterian Church, Cwmrhydyceirw, Morriston,1944.

Employees of the Ministry of Works depot at Cwmbwrla at their annual dinner and dance, held in Mumbles, 1947.

A welcome home from the war for this soldier, from friends and neighbours at Trallwn Road, Halfway, Llansamlet, late 1940s.

Members of Swansea Aero-modellers Club held their annual presentation dinner at the Bush Hotel, High Street, 1949. Before them, some of the trophies they competed for during the year.

Watch repairers and jewellers from Swansea who were among founder members of the British Horological Institute. They gathered in the city during the early 1950s with representatives of the watch-making factory at Ystradgynlais.

Almost a fashion parade of the immediate post war years — a family poses for the photographer outside their home in Watkin Street, Mount Pleasant, 1950.

Some of the main guests at the annual dinner of Swansea Licensed Victuallers Association, 1950.

Whatever was grabbing their attention had generated a near full house at Pontardawe Public Hall, a cinema and concert venue, when this picture was taken from its balcony, 1950.

Some of the members of Swansea Womens' Guild at the Municipal Club, Heathfield, early 1950s.

Members of the Sisterhood of Alexandra Road Presbyterian Church, before attending a rally, mid-1950s.

A group of friends at the Patti Pavilion, Christmas Eve, 1959.

Watched by the licensee, staff and other thirsty customers, one of the regulars prepares to cut a ceremonial ribbon to signify the first Sunday opening of The Park Hotel, Portland Street, along with other pubs in Swansea, November 12, 1961.

Some of the lads enjoy a pint to celebrate that historic Sunday opening milestone inside The Park Hotel, November 12, 1961.

Members of the cricket team at Hodges Menswear factory, Fforestfach, during their annual dinner, March 1964.

Members of Swansea School Caretakers Association gather for their annual dinner, at the Dolphin Hotel, Whitewalls, 1964.

Swansea Docks' supervisors at their annual dinner in the Langland Court Hotel, November 1964.

Firemen celebrate the retirement of colleague, station officer Fred Trew, front row, second left, from Swansea Fire Service, 1966. The function was held at the Municipal Club, Heathfield.

Presentation of a TV to Hill House Hospital, May 1968. It was bought with the proceeds of a theatrical revue performed by staff of Lewis Lewis department store, High Street.

Swansea couple Edward and Audrey Morris were successful contestants on TV's popular quiz programme Mr & Mrs in 1980. Here they are seen with the show's host Alan Taylor and a hostess.

Planting of a tree in Castle Gardens to mark the official twinning of Swansea with the German city of Mannheim, late 1960s.

Charles Dilley, president of Swansea Rotary Club surrounded by members of Swansea Model Agency at a fund-raising fashion show held at the Top Rank, The Kingsway, 1979. Looking on is a fellow Rotarian.

Members of Swansea Inner Wheel Club at the group's Oxford Street charity shop, late 1980s.

Members of Townhill and Mayhill Camera Club at an annual awards evening, mid-1970s.

Staff and friends of Clydach Hospital gather around the 'Guess The Weight of the Cake' stall at its 1986 annual fete.

Drivers of Cambrian United Dairies, later Unigate, at a safe driving award ceremony held at the Pines Hotel, Treboeth, early 1970s.

SUBURBAN SPOTLIGHT

Much of Manselton was simply an open space when this 1914 photograph was taken from the Racecourse. The centre of the panorama is dominated by Manselton school and to the left, St Michael's Church. The chimneys of Cwmfelin works in the background.

Gwydr Terrace, early 1900s. It was later renamed Uplands Crescent.

Brynymor Road looking towards St Helen's Road, 1910.

The old road and the new, above, at Kittle Hill, looking towards Bishopston, early 1920s.

Singleton Abbey, which has grown into Swansea University, as it was in the mid-1920s.

Singleton Lodge, Brynmill, viewed from Mumbles Road on a summer's day 1920.

Uplands Crescent, showing Waynes' Stores and florists, mid-1920s. Parking seems to have been much easier then if of course you didn't arrive on one of the trams that ran on the rails visible in the roadway.

Foxhole Post Office, St Thomas, with postmistress Audrey Featherstone outside, 1935.

Bomb damaged houses in Sketty Road, Uplands, a sign that Swansea had been visited by the German Luftwaffe bombers in wartime 1941.

A solitary swan punctuates this tranquil view of Brynmill Park, 1956.

Construction of local authority housing at
Heol Gwyrosydd, Penlan, 1948. The houses
were built by apprentices under the highly
successful Rimmer scheme.

Cascarinis Café, Fabian Street, St Thomas
with staff taking a rare break from their
labours, 1957.

Penlan school in the early stages of construction, 1954.

The sweeping arc of Wimmerfield Crescent makes it easily identifiable in this aerial view of Killay taken during April 1962.

Mynyddbach Girls School, May 1971.

Sway Road, Morriston, looking towards Ynystawe, May 1971.

Station Road, Cockett, January, 1973, looking towards the traffic lights at its junction with Cockett Road and Cwmbach Road.

Shops around the busy Fforestfach Square crossroads before demolition to enable road widening to take place, mid-1970s.

A view of St Thomas with Kilvey Hill in the background from the seaward quayside at Prince of Wales Dock, 1975. The spire of St. Thomas Church dominates the scene.

Church Road, Llansamlet, with the Plough and Harrow Inn, just visible in front of St Samlet's Church, 1975.

Roadway developments at Dyfatty, mid-1970s. This view was taken from the site of the former Dublin Arms, Bridge Street, looking towards Prince of Wales Road.

Clase Road, Morriston, looking eastwards, with Wychtree roundabout at the bottom of the hill and Llansamlet in the distant background, 1978.

Uplands Crescent shopping area struggles to get back to normal after a heavy snowfall, January, 1982.

Brynymor Road was among the victims of the January 1982 snowfall. This picture shows shoppers queuing for bread outside a bakery as loaves were in short supply.

The snowfall, in January 1982, left deep drifts throughout many Swansea's districts. This scene was captured in Armine Road, Fforestfach, with Gendros School in the background.

Astra jewellers shop had a commanding presence in Brynymor Road as this mid- 1980s picture shows.

The Patti Pavilion and St Helen's rugby and cricket ground feature in this mid 1980s view from the rooftop of the Guildhall showing the majestic sweep of Swansea Bay.

HAVING A PARTY

Young residents of Windmill Terrace, St Thomas on a carnival float during 1937.

Wounded wartime servicemen from Morriston Hospital were given a slap-up meal at Woolworth's High Street cafeteria by the store's staff, 1944.

A Christmas party in Llansamlet Parish Hall 1927

Residents of Campbell Street and Northill Road, Mount Pleasant, united for a party to celebrate VE-Day, September 1945.

Young and old residents of Tegid Road, Mayhill, at their VE-Day celebration party, 1945

Residents of Terrace Road, Mount Pleasant, out in force to celebrate the Festival of Britain, 1951.

Staff of the Lewis Lewis department store at High Street at the Mackworth Hotel during their 1951 Christmas party.

Residents of Glanyrafon Gardens, Sketty, celebrated the Coronation of Queen Elizabeth II at St Helen's rugby and cricket ground in June, 1953.

A welcome home party at Halfway, Llansamlet for one of the residents who had served in the Army during the Second World War, 1945.

A group of Mumbles friends at a fancy dress party in the village's Pier Hotel, 1953.

There were plenty of flags and banners stretched out across Rodney Street, Sandfields in June 1953 when its neighbours celebrated the Coronation of Queen Elizabeth II.

A Swansea family sits down to celebrate a 21st birthday – 1950s style.

This group of women enjoyed an evening of hi-jinks at the Municipal Club, Heathfield, in the mid-1950s.

Young Pontardawe steelworks office workers enjoy a works party at the town's Rink hall, 1950s.

Staff of Morsmith Motors at their annual Christmas party in the Mackworth Hotel, High Street, 1959.

Staff of Pontardawe steelworks let their hair down during a game of musical chairs at their annual dinner and dance at the Caswell Bay Hotel, Gower, on Tuesday, December 15, 1959.

A party in full swing at the Osborne Hotel, Langland, Tuesday, December 20, 1960.

Fancy dress was the order of the day for these members of Swansea Fire Service at the Pier Hotel, Mumbles, in the early 1960s.

Children from Swansea foster homes joined those of staff members when the Lewis Lewis store organised a Christmas party on December 7, 1967.

Staff of Hodges menswear factory, Fforestfach at an early 1960s get together.

A Christmas party organised for children of staff at the Lewis Lewis department store, High Street, 1968.

Neighbours of Aberdyberthi Street, Hafod celebrated the wedding of Prince Charles and Lady Diana by holding a fancy dress parade, July 1981. The winner was the youngster dressed as a Dutch girl on the front left.

Supervisory staff of the Northgate clothing factory, Kingsway industrial estate, Fforestfach at their Christmas party, late 1970s.

Women from the Northgate Group's clothing factory at Fforestfach industrial estate take time out from their labours to celebrate the Silver Jubilee of Queen Elizabeth II, 1977.

A Christmas party attended by the children of members of Swansea Male Voice Choir, late 1960s.

Some of the staff of Marks & Spencer, Oxford Street, during celebrations to mark the company's centenary, 1984.

SHOPPING SPREE

The interior of Swansea Market, 1906.

The original grocery and provisions premises of Wayne's Stores, Uplands Crescent, Uplands, Swansea, 1910.

In the early 1920s The Bon Marche shop at 1 Castle Square, was a noted destination for gifts. According to Fred S Morris, its proprietor, it had the largest stock of dolls and toys in Wales. There was also a constant supply of all the latest novelties.

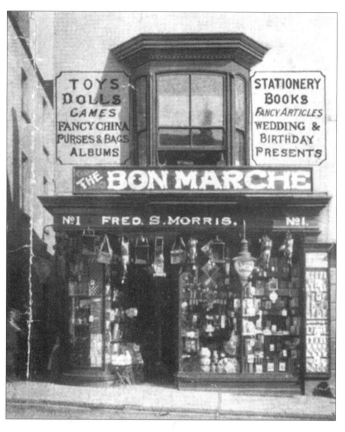

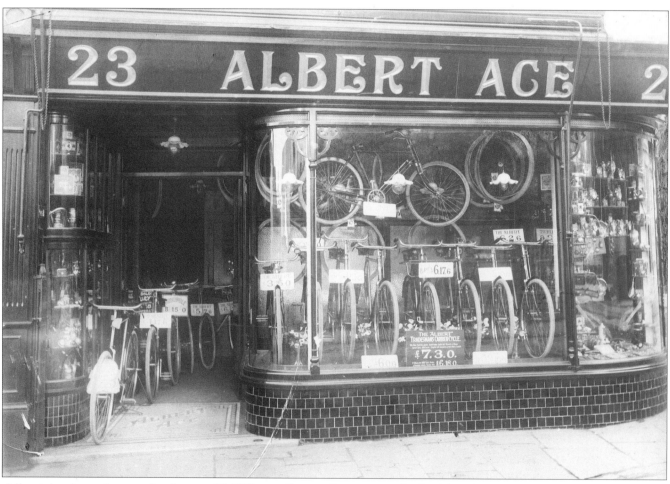

Albert Ace's cycle supply shop at 23 Dillwyn Street. It even stocked a bicycle named The Albert – on offer for a little over £6 when this picture was taken in 1922.

Staff of William Molyneux Fish Merchants High Street pictured outside the premises with the firm's delivery lorry, 1923. Next door to the left was Maggie Powe's sweet shop. The business was close to the junction of High Street and Greyhound Street.

This was the window display that won first prize for Albert Ace's Dillwyn Street cycle shop in a window dressing competition organised by The Trader magazine to celebrate National Cycle Week, May 28, 1923.

John Bull Stores, 1931. The shop stood in High Street, almost opposite the Palace Theatre. The message on the building's front wall says the store was a pioneer of cheap trading and believed in "small profits for quick returns."

SMALL
PROFITS
&
QUICK
RETURNS

PIONEE
OF
CHEA
TRADI

JOHN BULL STORE
CHEAPEST
GROCERS
IN TOWN

JOHN BULL STORES

CAKE 5ᴰ

PURE BUTTER 1/4 Pound

PURE LARD 8 Pound

S.R. FLOUR 2¼ Pound

Pears were just 2d each from the well-stocked fruit and veg barrow of Harry Barratt, wearing a bow tie in Oxford Street, early 1930s. He also had a stall in the market and frequently parked his barrow near the Slip Bridge, where trade was brisk on sunny days.

The well-stocked fresh fruit stall of D R Roberts in Swansea market, 1933.

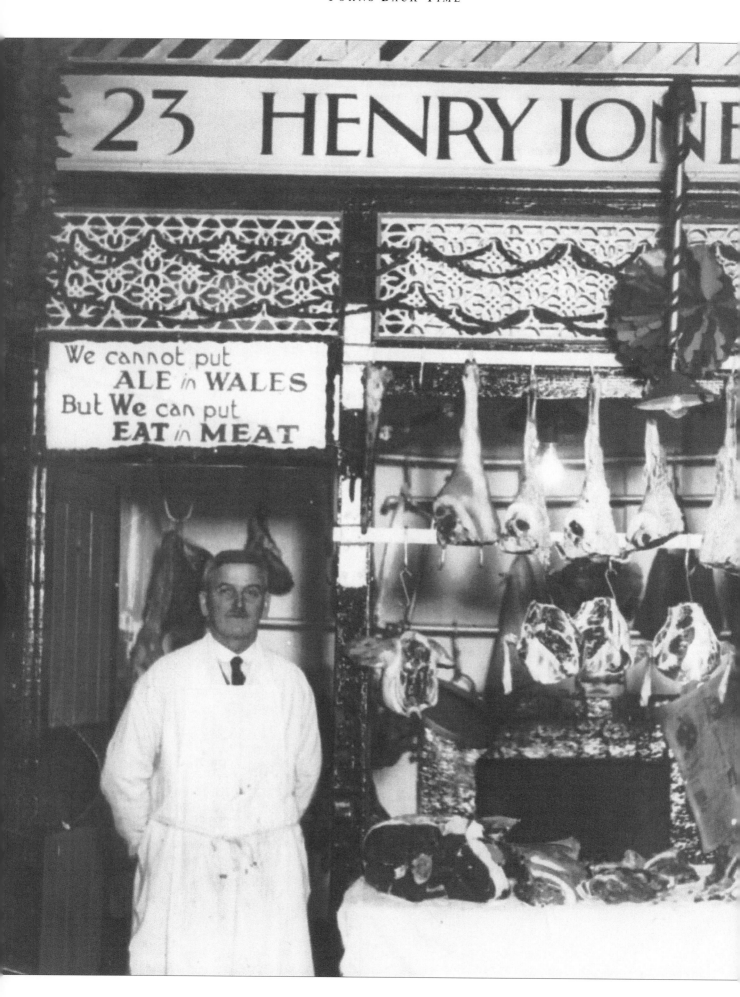

Henry Jones and his wife of Hunts Farm, Pennard, Gower, on the successful butchery stall they ran in Swansea market, late 1930s.

Handbag in tow it's off to the shops with granny for this little girl seen in St Helen's Road, opposite Argyle Chapel, 1949.

A typical Swansea shopper, in Castle Street, late 1940s. Woolworth's High Street store can be seen behind her.

The Astra Watch and Clock repair service's first shop, Argyle Street, 1945.

Proprietor Evan Mons Jones, outside Manor Bakery, Manselton, 1951.

What the well-dressed man wore when he hit town on a day off. This gent was spotted in Alexandra Road, with the railway station behind, 1949.

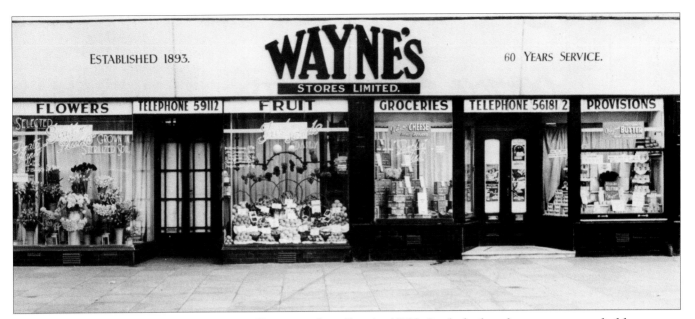

Wayne's Stores, Uplands, celebrating 60 years of trading in 1953. In their day they were regarded by many as the Fortnum and Masons of Swansea.

Staff of Loosemores tobacconists and confectionary shop, St Helen's Road, early 1960s.

True-Form was a familiar name to many shoe shoppers at one time. This was the company's shop in High Street, during the late 1950s.

The Caer Street florists of Robin Wayne, with two of its delivery vans outside. The Mini van in front had only just been launched, 1959.

Astra Jewellers had moved to new premises in Brynymor Road, when this picture was taken in 1959.

Pile 'em high and sell 'em cheap was the motto of Macphersons in Oxford Street, one of Swansea's first supermarket style grocery stores, pictured here in the late 1970s. Green Shield stamps provided the loyalty reward then.

Hot pants and high boots were all the rage when this late 1960s picture was taken inside an Oxford Street fashion boutique.

Henry Gooding and Co., supplied painting and decorating materials from their shop, seen here in 1963, on the corner of High Street and Greenhill Street. The building, long demolished, was just below today's busy Dyfatty crossroads.

The David Evans Department store, Princess Way on a summer's afternoon in the late 1970s.

A bustling Swansea Market with its fresh produce stalls, late 1980s.

THE YOUNG ONES

Seven sisters outside their home in Tymaen Street, Danygraig, 1909. The daughters of Maria Diamond, their names were Cybil, Lily, Gwynlais, Gladys, Doris, Maud and Florence. They also had three brothers – George, Cyril and Leonard.

Cub Scouts and Brownies near the Roman Bridge, Blackpill, about 1930.

A group of Girl Guides in the early 1930s while on a summer camp in Gower.

These girls were attending a birthday party for one of their friends at her home in Nicander Parade, Mayhill, 1933.

Roman Bridge, Blackpill provided a welcome resting point for these Girl Guides in the mid-1930s.

Queuing for the drinking fountain at Hafod Park, 1939. The little lad on the right hasn't much chance though!

A company of Girl Guides at a camp in the grounds of Penrice, Gower, 1937.

Youngsters gather to watch the action at Brynmill boating lake, 1938.

Discovering some of the magic of Christmas, early 1950s-style.

Participants in the first Holy Communion at Our Lady of Lourdes church, Townhill, 1952.

A Sunday School class at Ebenezer Gospel Hall, Heol-y-Gors, Cwmbwrla, October 28, 1945.

Cubs and Scouts of Plasmarl's Robin Hood troop help celebrate the 80th birthday of their group leader's mother, early 1950s.

Children of employees of the Richard Thomas & Baldwin steelworks at Pontardawe during a Christmas party, 1952.

There were plenty of Indian feather party hats in evidence at Townhill Nursery's 1952 Christmas celebration.

Youngsters take part in a Corpus Christi parade, June, 1955. They are seen on St Helen's Road, near its junction with Mumbles Road. The Slip Bridge stonework is in the background.

Members of the Saturday morning club at the Odeon cinema, Sketty, 1957. One thing is certain – they wouldn't have been watching the advertised film The Passionate Stranger. That was one for their parents.

Looking very smart in their finery, these young girls from Jones Terrace, Mount Pleasant are all dressed up for Whit Sunday, 1964.

Young guests at the Children's Hospital Ball, at the Brangwyn Hall, 1957.

Members of the Hill Chapel Sunday School, Northill Road, Mount Pleasant, 1970.

Cadle Youth Club members with leaders and guests after a presentation ceremony for achievement in the mid 1980s.

The steps of Mount Pleasant Chapel in The Kingsway was a popular meeting place for Swansea youngsters, especially on a school lunch hour as this 1965 picture shows.

All packed and ready to go — Fforestfach Brownies about to set off for their annual camp, 1984.

MUMBLES & GOWER

Mumbles village viewed from the South, near the pier entrance, late 1880s.

A busy scene at Mumbles Road, Southend, near the Dunns, early 1900s. The Mumbles Pharmacy on the right is now Boots the Chemists.

Looking across Langland Bay, early 1900s.

Caswell Bay, early 1900s. A windmill is just visible on the distant headland.

Parkmill village, presents a tranquil scene, 1905

Mumbles lighthouse and the new road to Limeslade, 1908.

Now one of Swansea's busiest traffic intersections, this was Sketty Cross in 1910.

The village school at Parkmill, 1910.

Oxwich Church, nestling
among the trees close to
the sea, 1910.

Motor dealer Tom Hutchins was selling Fordson tractors for
£280 at his Gower Show stand, 1910.

Llechryd Hill,
Gower, 1911.

The gardens, at Southend, in the
summer of 1915.

Bathing machines on the sands at Langland Bay. It's landmark beach huts had yet to make their presence felt, 1916.

The Langland Bay Hotel stands a magnificent sentinel over its surroundings, 1918.

A steam-hauled Mumbles train halts at Oystermouth station, early 1920s.

Holiday bungalows at Plunch Lane, Limeslade, mid-1920s.

Smales tea rooms and ice cream cabin at Langland, 1922.

Taking a dip at Langland, mid-1920s.

Rotherslade Bay, looking towards Langland, mid-1920s.

Mumbles Pier and Lifeboat station, early 1920s.

Pennard Castle's walls offer a welcome windbreak to a troop of Girl Guides during a Gower hike, 1937.

The Parade and Gardens, Southend with a Mumbles Railway car in the background, early 1930s.

The cutting at Mumbles, late 1940s.

Pwll Du Bay, 1938. Access to the house on the beach presented plenty of problems for owners down the decades.

The path along the clifftop towards Langland, late 1940s.

A view across Norton, back towards Swansea across the bay, late 1940s.

The shelter at Rotherslade Bay, early 1950s.

Beware the dog! This giant fibreglass corgi seen in 1973 may not have been able to bite, but it certainly made its presence felt for many years in Plunch Lane, Bracelet Bay.

Langland Bay, August bank holiday, 1983.

The Osborne Hotel overlooking Rotherslade Bay, August, 1983.

A unique panorama of Langland, with its rows of
beach huts and, tucked in to the right, tiny Rotherslade
Bay with its shelter, 1973.

MUSIC & MOVEMENT

The Salvation Army's Swansea Citadel Junior Band, 1947.

Cast members of The Man Who Changed His Name performed by Soar Chapel Fforestfach, at the Welfare Hall, on February 23 and 24, 1939.

Some of the dancers who took part in Swansea Amateur Operatic Society's performance of The Desert Song at the Empire Theatre, 1948.

Participants in the York Place Chapel Gang Show, 1950.

Children of Rhyddings United Reformed Church, Brynmill during a pantomime staged at Rhyddings Church Hall, 1960.

Members of Swansea Amateur Operatic Society who took part in the musical Showboat at the Grand Theatre during the mid-1960s.

Sunday school members of St James' Church, Walter Road who staged a successful play, 1965.

Len Dymond, a regular and popular pianist at the ICI Club, 1963.

The Lewis Lewis department store theatre group on stage in 1964.

Pupils of Brynhyfryd School during rehearsals for the school play, late 1960s.

The drama group of the Lewis Lewis store during a 1968 production.

Banging a drum in celebration of the Investiture of the Prince of Wales in July 1969 are children from Graig Terrace, Mount Pleasant.

The Singing Barmen who had crowds flocking to The Canopic restaurant, Mumbles, in 1970.

Members of Swansea Male Voice Choir off on a trip to Swansea's twin town of Mannheim, Germany, early 1970s.

Participants from the many Scout and Guide organisations who took part in a Gang Show at the Grand Theatre, 1970.

Members of the Midnite Sound, a successful Swansea club and function band which delighted audiences across South Wales during the 1970s.

Top Swansea ballroom dancing duo David and Gay Mitchell, 1973.

Vocal harmony band Curly, a popular musical act with Swansea audiences, 1972.

These youngsters played the Von Trapp children in a production of The Sound of Music staged by Gendros Catholic Amateur Operatic Society in 1982 at the Grand Theatre, Swansea. Among them, top right is none other than modern day superstar Catherine Zeta Jones. Her young co-stars for this early performance included Wayne Eaton, Liz Rebecca Lloyd, Simon Davies, Helen Jones and Sandra Morris.

The Windsor Four performing at Llansamlet Social Club, 1975.

TRANSPORT & TRAVEL

This vehicle carries the first registration number used in Swansea – CY1. Pictured on a vehicle in the early 1900s, this is however, not necessarily the first vehicle registered in the city.

This Clements-make early motorcycle was used by a Swansea family in 1905. It carries an early Swansea registration – CY 56.

Another early motorcycle used in Swansea — an Ormonde-make two and a quarter horse power, machine, 1902.

An early one horse power Werner motorcycle receives some attention from its Swansea rider while a family watch, 1901.

These rare pictures show brave aviator Ernie Sutton making the first flight ever by an aircraft in Glamorgan. They were taken on January 23, 1911, the day he took off from Oxwich beach in a Bleriot single-engine monoplane.

Right: Curious villagers inspect the Bleirot XI aeroplane on Oxwich sands, while a group of pilot Ernie Sutton's supporters engage in conversation.

Bottom left: A final handshake for Sutton – a Swansea motor trader with premises in Dillwyn Street – before take off. By today's standards he seems ill-dressed for such an epic adventure, and looks nothing if not a little apprehensive.

Bottom centre: Back firmly on the ground after the maiden Glamorgan – flight? Not quite, Sutton is chaired aloft by his supporters. His history-making complete.

Bottom right: A minor mishap. One of Sutton's subsequent flights ended when the aircraft plunged nose first into the sand.

This fascinating glimpse of bus travel in its infancy shows a Daimler six horsepower, two cylinder tube ignition vehicle with the name Swansea Motor Bus Co., Ltd., emblazoned on its side. The vehicle had four forward and four reverse gears and is seen parked outside the Mermaid Hotel, Mumbles in 1905. The passengers waiting to make their journey, possibly into Swansea were a worthy bunch. They included: H A Chapman, renowned town photographer; John Morris, coroner and solicitor; Ernest Leeder, estate agent, accompanied by his two daughters; Penrose Thomas, coal exporter; R E Jones, hotel proprietor; Dick Ashley, driver; Viner Leeder, solicitor; Arthur Burt, also a hotel proprietor and Alfred Davies, tobacconist.

A four cylinder Bedford 12 horsepower car passes a lone horseman on Mumbles Road, 1907. Cars were quickly becoming popular – the registration of this one is CY 906. *Right,* a close-up of the same car.

Mr W Pryce Trow of Swansea, and his family in a 12 HP Aster two cylinder vehicle, registration number CY 6, out for a run, 1904.

The first bus to begin a regular service to Llangenith, 1910.

Two early Swansea cars – on the left a Scripps Booth, and on the right a Maxwell. The picture was taken in Walter Road, in the early 1920s.

The steam-hauled Mumbles train passes under the Slip bridge, heading out of town, 1920.

A mixed bag of early Swansea-owned vehicles lined up during the mid-1920s.

Hundreds of passengers clamber aboard the Mumbles train, heading for an afternoon out at the pier, around 1910. Behind them are some of the goods sidings for Swansea Victoria railway station.

An unique transport scene – A Swansea tram meets up with the Mumbles train at the junction of St Helen's Road and Oystermouth Road around 1910. A petrol driven lorry transporting Bowen's mineral water can be seen alongside.

If you ordered groceries from Wayne's stores, Uplands Crescent, Uplands, in the 1930s then it is quite likely that it would have been delivered to your door in this van, seen parked in the lane behind the premises.

Two Swansea women, out for a jaunt in a Bull Nose Morris Cowley car, are pictured near Brandy Cove, Gower, 1930

A Corona pop lorry delivers to Lon Coed Bran, Uplands in the mid-1950s. The houses behind it are in Lon Ger y Coed.

Coach operator E G Jones of Danygraig always called his latest vehicle The Lark. At least that's how the story goes. This one was his pride and joy in the late 1940s. If you were lucky you could join one of the firms two or three day tours on such a coach.

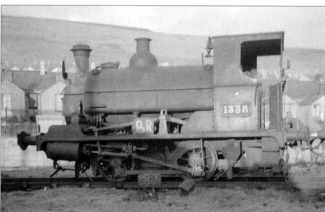

Two unusual steam locomotives at Swansea's East Dock depot in August 1962. They had both been operated by British Rail and the Great Western Railway before being handed down for shunting work around Swansea Docks, where they finished their days.

A fleet of Morris 1000 vans operated by Swansea florists Robin Wayne lined up for the photographer on Mumbles Road in front of Singleton Lodge, early 1960s. Such a picture would be impossible today because of the volume of traffic on this major city road link.

Deliveries from the David Evans Food Hall, Princess Way were made in two BMC two ton diesel-powered vans like this one pictured in September, 1964. They each had dedicated delivery runs.

A BMC 30 cwt diesel delivery van that covered most of the southern half of Wales for Bailey's Broadloom Carpets, The Kingsway, 1964.

A line-up of Post Office telegram delivery riders on the last day of the service's operation, 1971.

A United Welsh bus company double decker pulls out of Singleton Street terminus – now Wilkinson's store – in the mid-1950s.

It was a sad day in 1983 for the driver of this lorry owned by long established Swansea removal firm Griff Fender. The vehicle was being prepared for its last loaded trip to London where it was to be scrapped. The return journey was made by a Pickfords vehicle, the national firm having taken over the local one. The picture was taken outside the firm's Upper Bank depot in Swansea Enterprise Park.

Pontardawe-based Hutchins Coaches carried people from all over the Swansea Valley on trips far and wide for many years. These are some of the vehicles they operated in the late 1970s.

The maintenance van used by Astra jewellers, of Brynymor Road, 1962.

A CLASS ACT

Standard 7, Cwmbwrla Girls' School, 1919.

Standard 1, Terrace Road Infants', 1919.

A young class at St Thomas Infants School, behind their desks 1924.

A class at Sketty School, Carnglas Road, 1924.

Class 1, St Thomas Infants School, 1925.

Standard 4, Peniel Green
Council School,
Llansamlet, 1924.

A class at Bethel Infants School, Llansamlet, 1937.

A group of five-year-olds dutifully wash their hands at Christchurch Infants School, Sandfields, 1949.

Morning assembly at Swansea Technical Secondary School, 1947.

Pupils from St Andrew's private school, Eaton Crescent, Swansea, 1950.

A class from Brynhyfryd
Boys School, early 1950s.

Some of the pupils of Clwyd School, Penlan, June 1954.

Form 4B Powys Junior School, Powys Avenue, Townhill, 1955. The Phoenix Centre now stands on this site.

Class 4A, Oxford Street School, 1955.

Form 3, Glanmor Secondary School for Girls, 1955.

Pupils of Brynhyfryd Junior Mixed School, summer 1958.

A class at Terrace Road Primary School, 1959, pictured with their teacher and Leonard Davies, headteacher.

Form 2C Clwyd School, June 1956.

Girls of Ceiriog House, St Helen's Secondary Modern School, Sandfields, on St David's Day, 1959.

Pupils of Manselton Primary School dressed up for their International Day, 1961.

A class at Manselton Infants School, St David's Day, 1962.

Some of the pupils of Brynmill Infants
School, April 1965.

A class at Brynhyfryd Junior School, prepare
for a trip to Scandanavia aboard the educational
cruise ship MS Devonia, May 1966.

It was a case of lessons with a difference on the day these pupils of St Thomas Junior School took their pets along in 1967.

Pupils at St Thomas Junior School, 1966.

Class 4A Brynmill Junior Mixed School, 1967.

A civic lesson for these pupils of
Brynhyfryd School in 1966
when mayor of Swansea
Councillor Frank Jones joined
them one morning.

A class at Bishopston Junior School,
1970.

Pupils of Clase Junior School, Morriston, 1974 with their teacher and headteacher.

Classes J2A and J3, Pennard County Primary School, 1978.

The reception class at Gendros Primary School, 1978.

Class J32, Gors Junior School, 1979.

Form 6-0, Morriston Comprehensive School, 1979.

The choir of Mynyddbach Girls' School which won the choral competition when the Royal National Eisteddfod of Wales was held at Singleton, June 6, 1981.

WORK FORCE

Workers on number one shift at the Superheater Units munitions factory, The Strand, August, 1916.

The proprietors and staff of Morriston Star Laundry, 1922.

A fascinating glimpse of the inside of Lloyds Bank, Temple Street, 1933. The building was destroyed in the Three Nights Blitz by German Luftwaffe bombers during February 1941.

These miners took part in a BBC radio religious broadcast from the underground chapel at Mynydd Newydd colliery, Penlan, on Sunday, October 13, 1929.

Mayor Sir William Jenkins with other civic dignitaries visit Conway Road, Penlan, in 1947 to inspect progress on the Swansea Building Apprentices Scheme. The apprentices, some of whom are pictured were involved in the Rimmer home building scheme.

Husband and wife team Arthur and Ruth Richards, caretakers of Mayhill School in the late 1930s.

A group of apprentices who worked on Swansea's Rimmer local authority house building scheme at Heol Gwyrosydd, Penlan, 1948. They are pictured with foreman Bill Giltenan.

Staff of Richard Thomas & Baldwin's Pontardawe steelworks at their Ynisderw Road office, early 1950s.

Two sisters hard at work behind the bar of the Cwmbwrla Inn, their home, in the 1950s. They were Rose Pomford and Florence Williams.

Employees of the paint shop at the Louis Marx toy factory, Fforestfach, November 1948.

Workmen from the British Electrical Repairs depot at Neath Road, Hafod, 1950.

Women employees of Hodges Menswear factory at Fforestfach, 1950.

Cwmfelin steelworks, with its three stacks, affectionately known by nearby residents and employees as The Three Sisters, 1951.

Women employees at the Louis Marx toy factory, Fforestfach, June 1951.

Washing buses at South Wales Transport's busy Ravenhill depot, late 1950s.

Staff at the Prestcold refrigerator factory at Jersey Marine, late 1950s. The plant was eventually taken over by the Ford Motor Company for the production of driveshafts and axles and is currently run under their Visteon motor parts banner.

A Cambrian United Dairies driver collecting milk churns from Gower farms, 1958.

Mechanics at the Gloucester Place garage of Rootes dealers Oscar Chess, provide some attention for the engine of a Hillman saloon, 1962.

Ready to pull the first pint at the new Swansea Dockers Club, St Thomas, 1966.

Domestic staff at Singleton Hospital, early 1960s.

Staff of the Hopkin Morgan bakery at Sway Road, Morriston, 1964.

Women employees of Corker and Bevan, Hafod, 1970.

Long term bus and coach driver Ron Hutchins, of Clydach, known to his friends as Roy, proudly displays the countless badges he was awarded for safe driving and an Evening Post placard proclaiming that he had driven more than two million miles, 1986.

Kitchen staff at Bishop Vaughan Comprehensive School, December 1971.

Mr Cyril Bowlie Evans, Swansea's Superintendent Registrar, who married more than 12,000 couples. This picture was taken on Boxing Day 1976 after he performed his last ceremony.

A gathering of employees of the David Evans department store, Princess Way in 1984. They had each clocked up more than 10 years service.

Gay Mitchell at work as an engraver at the family owned firm of Astra Jewellers, Brynymor Road, 1981.

Women catering staff from Townhill kitchen which prepared lunchtime meals for schools in a wide area of Swansea, October 1986.

TAKING A BREAK

Swansea Beach, near The Slip bridge was a popular summer venue when this view looking back towards the docks was captured in the early 1920s.

Pleasure flights were a huge attraction for visitors to Swansea Beach in the early 1920s. The problem was that aircraft like this Avro bi-plane could only take off and land when tidal conditions were right.

A group of day trippers about to set off for a charabanc excursion from outside the Atkinson Sports Shop, Oxford Street, in the early 1920s.

A group of Cwmbwrla residents all set for a paddle steamer excursion, June 5, 1930.

Setting off from The River Tawe for a paddle steamer trip across the Bristol Channel to Ilfracombe, 1926.

A 1937 outing from Swansea Naval and Military Club, Somerset Place. In those days the club was a 'men only' institution and this annual trip was the only concession they made to their wives, partners and children.

Employees of wholesalers Fred Morgan on a trip to Weston-Super-Mare, 1946.

Taking a break at the White Hart Inn, Llanddarog are men from the Hodges factory, Fforestfach on their annual day out, 1948.

Staff of the Ben Evans department store ready to board the coach that was to take them to Llandrindod Wells for their annual day out in 1948.

A busman's holiday? Probably, because these employees of South Wales Transport simply clambered aboard a coach for their annual day out, 1949.

Members and officers of Swansea High Street Salvation Army Corps gathered in front of Thomas Row before setting off for a day out in the late 1940s.

The paddle boats on Brynmill Park lake were a popular attraction. These two youngsters are enjoying the experience in the early 1950s.

Redundant aircraft fuel tanks were used to construct the rudimentary catamarans that provided the watery adventures at Singleton Park boating lake, early 1950s.

Some of the staff of Woolworths, High Street store were joined by a group of employees of the nearby Mackworth Hotel for this early 1950s coach trip.

Regulars of the Crown Inn, Morriston, prepare to set off on a coach trip to Blackpool, in the summer of 1950

Members of Swansea and District Motor Traders Asociation who visited Fort Dunlop, Birmingham on Monday June 4, 1951.

Employees of the Rediffusion shop, St Helen's Road, their families and friends, head off to Weston-Super-Mare, 1951.

A welcome break from their labours for employees of the Smiths Crisps factory at Fforestfach, early 1950s.

When the staff of the J&P Bevan garage posed for this 1952 picture they had no idea what lay ahead. Their destination was Lynmouth in Devon, which they never reached because of serious flooding that engulfed the town.

Staff of builders Lesley Davies, and their families headed off in the rain for this annual excursion in the late 1950s.

Management and staff of James Brothers drapers, High Street, in front of the coach that carried them off for a day out in 1960.

Llandrindod Wells was the destination for these employees of Lewis Lewis, the High Street department store, 1962.

Residents of Western Street, Sandfields, on a trip to Blackpool, early 1960s.

Employees of florists Robin Wayne, heading off for a day out in Holland and a trip to the bulb fields, 1970. They were joined by friends – and even some of the staff of Bateman Travel, Castle Street, as it was one of the first occasions when such a round trip had been attempted in just one day.

Members of Dyfatty Senior Citizens Club all set for a summer outing, early 1970s.

PLAYING THE GAME

Swansea Town AFC, 1923-24 season.

Members and officials of Swansea United Flying, Tippler and Tumbler Society at the end of their 1925 season.

Competitors in a motorcycle scramble held at Penllergaer, May 31, 1930.

Danygraig School football XI, 1947-48 season.

St Joseph's Primary School rugby XV, 1929.

Swansea Building Apprentices after their appearance in the Swansea Intermediate League Cup Final at Vetch Field, 1947. This was the first season that the team had been in existence. All the players were engaged in the apprentice building scheme. They included three carpenters, three bricklayers, three plasters and two plumbers.

Terrace Road Primary School rugby squad with the trophy they won on becoming champions in the primary schools competition, 1948-49.

Motorcycle ace Jack Daniels in high speed cornering action, 1948.

Swansea motorcycle ace Jack Daniels astride one of the machines that carried him to glory in 1948.

Pentrepoeth Senior School's A football team 1948-49.

Cwmbwrla Boys School, undefeated Swansea Schools Junior Cricket League Champions, 1949. They won their last game of the season, against St Joseph's, by the tightest margin of just one run.

Cage bird fancier Jack Hopping, of Ysgol Street, Port Tennant, proudly displays some of his many trophies, with his wife and daughters, early 1950s.

Cwmrhydyceirw Youth football team — winners of the West Wales Under 18s cup in 1951.

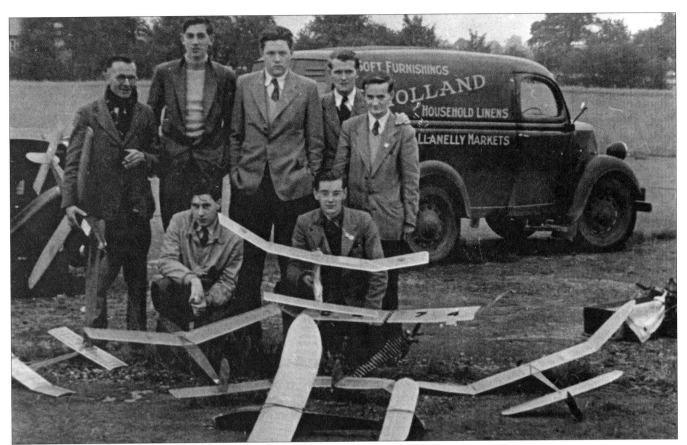

Some of the members of Swansea Aero Modelling Club during a 1951 competition.

On August 5 And 6, 1951 the British National aero-model flying competition was held at Fairwood Common. Here Lady Whitten-Brown, wife of aviation pioneer Sir Arthur Whitten-Brown presents a prize to one of the winners, Mr G Harris.

A group of footballers at Bonymaen, 1951.

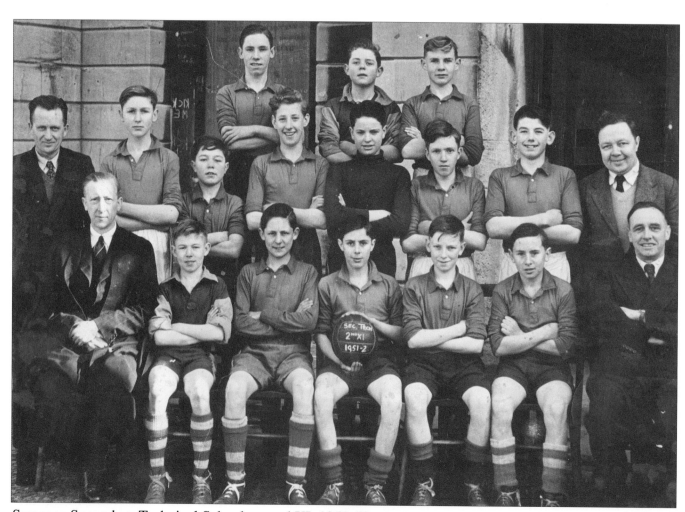

Swansea Secondary Technical School second XI, 1951-52 season.

Dynevor School rugby XV, 1951-52 season.

Stepney, Cwmbwrla XI after losing the Nursery Cup Final to the Welsh Juniors 1-0 at Bala, 1957.

Swansea soccer star brothers Mel Charles, left, and John Charles, right, shake hands as captains of their respective teams, Swansea and Leeds, before a capacity 29,000 crowd at Vetch Field in October, 1955. The Division Two encounter ended in a 1 – 1 draw. It was one of the few occasions when the brothers met as opponents.

Trevor Ford, left, and Ivor Allchurch, right, shake hands before kick off in the Welsh Cup Final between Cardiff City and Swansea Town, on April 30, 1956. Looking on is referee Mervyn Griffiths who was taking charge of his last big game.

The hockey team at Glanmor Secondary School for Girls, 1959.

Unit Cricket XI, 1959 winners of the Industrial League championship. Only one of the team's 11 members did not work for the Unit Superheater works in the Strand.

Portmead Junior Schools football squad, 1960.

The football squad formed from employees of Gregor Bros. timber merchants, 1960.

Officials and players of Hafod Brotherhood AFC with the four trophies they won in the 1960-61 season.

Cwm Glas School junior rugby team, 1962 completed an excellent debut season in the local schools league by finishing as runners up in the championship and sharing the Swansea Schools Cup. The boy holding the ball is Cyril Hartson, father of Wales and Glasgow Celtic striker John Hartson.

Portmead Primary School football team at Cwmbwrla Park, 1963.

Swansea Post Office rugby XV, 1965.

Swansea Otters Swimming Club, 1965.

Morriston Town AFC, 1965-66.

Plasmarl AFC – with mascot –
1971-72 season.

Presentation of trophies to Hafod
Brotherhood AFC, early 1980s.

Successful competitors in the netball
competition that was part of a late
1970s sports day at Olchfa
Comprehensive School.

Swansea City fans salute the success of their footballing heroes when they jammed St Helen's Road as the team were driven through the city after winning promotion to the First Division of the football league, 1981.

CLOCKING ON

No book entitled Swansea Turns Back Time would be complete without
a look at some of the public timepieces that help keep the city punctual.
Here are just a few captured by the camera down the years.

The clock in the tower of Tabernacle Chapel,
Morriston.

The floral clock at Victoria Park, during the
mid-1920s.

The location of this timepiece needs no explanation. It is of course at the entrance to Mumbles Pier.

Another, later view of the floral clock in Victoria Park flower gardens near the slip bridge. This one commemorates the Golden Jubilee of the Guide Dogs for the Blind organisation. Interestingly Swansea's floral clock is one of the few in the United Kingdom which has its hands planted with flowers. This picture shows the clock in all its glory in 1981. The clock mechanism was plucked from unintentional destruction by workmen preparing the foundation for a new car park, early in 2004.

Standing tall and proud – the clock tower of Swansea Guildhall.

The clock in the tower that once stood outside the Co-op store at Penplas. It was removed after the building was destroyed by fire. This clock had originally been part of Ravenhill Bowls Pavilion until that too was destroyed by fire in 1978.

City clock repairer David Mitchell at work on the familiar rooftop timepiece of the former British Transport Docks Board offices in Adelaide Street. The building is now the five-star Morgan's Hotel.

This clock built into the façade of Treboeth Public Hall was refurbished and replaced during the 1980s.

The clock tower of the former Swansea General Hospital, retained in the retirement apartments that now occupy the St Helen's Road, site.

A rare view inside the clock that overlooks Orchard Street and Alexandra Road as part of the tower above the former Swansea Central Police Station. It is being wound by clock expert David Mitchell, who was responsible for refurbishing it.